AF735075

Susanna Bennett is a barrister at Deka Chambers. She specialises in the law of clinical negligence and acts for both claimants and defendants. The 2024 edition of the Legal 500 names her as a rising star in clinical negligence, describing her as follows: "Susanna is not only very clever but she has excellent judgement. She is one to watch."

A Practical Guide to the Non-Delegable Duty of Care in Healthcare

A Practical Guide to the Non-Delegable Duty of Care in Healthcare

Susanna Bennett

Barrister, Gray's Inn

Law Brief Publishing

© Susanna Bennett

All rights reserved. No part of this publication may be reproduced, stored in a retrieval system, or transmitted, in any form or by any means, electronic, mechanical, photocopying, recording or otherwise, without the prior permission of the publisher.

Excerpts from judgments and statutes are Crown copyright. Any Crown Copyright material is reproduced with the permission of the Controller of OPSI and the King's Printer for Scotland. Some quotations may be licensed under the terms of the Open Government Licence (http://www.nationalarchives.gov.uk/doc/open-government-licence/version/3).

Cover image © iStockphoto.comMartinPrescott

The information in this book was believed to be correct at the time of writing. All content is for information purposes only and is not intended as legal advice. No liability is accepted by either the publisher or author for any errors or omissions (whether negligent or not) that it may contain. Professional advice should always be obtained before applying any information to particular circumstances.

Published 2024 by Law Brief Publishing, an imprint of Law Brief Publishing Ltd
30 The Parks
Minehead
Somerset
TA24 8BT

www.lawbriefpublishing.com

Paperback: 978-1-916698-34-5

PREFACE

Thanks to Tim Kevan and Garry Wright at Law Brief Publishing for suggesting that I write a book on the non-delegable duty of care in healthcare. It has proved an interesting topic! I have enjoyed thinking about it from different angles and working through what practitioners in the field would find most useful. All turns on what is absolutely a legal question (is a non-delegable duty of care owed?), but the context is a messy, factual one, defined by how healthcare (and healthcare indemnity!) is provided in England. (Let me apologise now for confining myself to England.) Once the authorities are understood, and the facts properly analysed, the conclusion regarding whether there is a non-delegable duty of care sometimes becomes clear. But oftentimes it does not, and that is where I hope this book will come in handy, in helping practitioners identify the key legal principles, work out whether further information is needed, and finally determine the strength of their client's stance on this point and whether it is worth running the matter to a trial. This is intended to be a short introduction to the topic. I hope it fits the bill.

I have sought to state the law as at 30 April 2024. It goes without saying that this work may contain mistakes, despite my best efforts. I assume no responsibility for errors, inaccuracies, omissions or any other inconsistencies within it, and disclaim liability to any party for loss or damage as a result of reliance on the same. Please seek expert legal advice.

I have practised at the Bar since 2018 and joined 1 Chancery Lane (now the revamped merged set Deka Chambers) in 2019. I practised in clinical negligence from the start, and this area has come (intentionally) to occupy the majority of my practice, because I find it particularly interesting. I had my first real introduction to the intellectual challenge of non-delegable duties in healthcare in 2020 when I worked with Simon Readhead KC on a major case in the field. Thank you Simon. Throughout my time at the Bar I have been blessed to be surrounded by excellent colleagues at what is now Deka Chambers (not all of them clinical negligence specialists). There are too many to thank individually, but particular thanks to Laura Johnson KC, Jack Harding, Tom Collins, Dominique Smith and Anirudh Mandagere, all of whom have been hugely supportive, encouraging, wise and generous with their time. I could not have done it without them.

Susanna Bennett
May 2024

CONTENTS

CHAPTER ONE

INTRODUCTION

The existence of non-delegable duties of care has become a key battleground in clinical negligence claims in recent years. This is because of the increase in contracting out NHS-funded care to private companies, combined with the (recently vigorously reaffirmed[1]) limits to vicarious liability for independent contractors. It reflects claimants' concerns that potential defendants may not be financially sound (usually due to inadequate insurance arrangements), and their wish to pin liability on a defendant with broad shoulders (typically a public body).

It has long been understood, as stated in obiter dicta in many leading cases, that the organisation running a hospital owes a non-delegable duty of care to patients admitted to the hospital. This was reaffirmed (obiter) in *Woodland v Swimming Teachers Association and ors*[2], still the leading case on non-delegable duties at common law, which introduced Lord Sumption's familiar five defining features of a non-delegable duty. The Court of Appeal case of *Hughes v Rattan*[3] applied this five-stage test to a dental practice and found that the owner of the practice owed its patients a non-delegable duty. The case confirmed, if confirmation were needed, that arguments about the existence of a

1 By the Supreme Court in *Barclays Bank Plc v Various Claimants* [2020] UKSC 13; [2020] A.C. 973

2 [2013] UKSC 66; [2014] A.C. 537

3 [2022] EWCA Civ 107; [2022] 1 W.L.R. 1680

non-delegable duty are now central to bringing and defending claims arising from medical care in all different settings.

This book is written for lawyers. It is intended to be an overview of the law of non-delegable duties of care, whether arising at common law or under statute; an analysis of the rationale for applying them to medical care; a brief introduction to the organisation of the NHS, outsourcing of care, and indemnity cover; a guide to arguments which can be advanced for and against the existence of a non-delegable duty in a range of likely scenarios; and practical tips on litigating non-delegable duties. It is thus a short and non-exhaustive introduction for lawyers to the legal and theoretical underpinnings of, practical purpose for, and guidance on litigating, non-delegable duties in medical care.

CHAPTER TWO

WHAT IS A NON-DELEGABLE DUTY OF CARE?

A non-delegable duty of care is a duty for which the principal retains legal responsibility, even if its actual performance is delegated. If the person to whom performance has been delegated fails to perform the duty with reasonable care the principal will be liable for the breach, even if not personally at fault. It contrasts with the ordinary duty of care, which is discharged if reasonable care is taken in selecting a third party to carry it out.

It has been called a "personal" duty because the principal cannot pass on the legal responsibility. It is thus a form of strict liability, because it is imposed on the principal without a need for the principal to be at fault.

A non-delegable duty is for our purposes a duty to take reasonable care: its precise content depends at common law on the relationship which forms its basis, and, for a statutory non-delegable duty, on interpretation of the words of the statutory provision which establishes it.

It appears, but is not the subject of binding case law, that a non-delegable duty of care can be breached by a deliberate wrong: see *Armes v Nottinghamshire County Council*[4] at paragraph 51.

The paradigm example of a common law non-delegable duty is the duty of care owed by an employer to its employees: a duty to take reasonable care to keep its employees safe from reasonably foreseeable risks of harm. Thus, an employer which delegates to a third party the task of organising a safe system of work will be liable if the third party is negligent in carrying this out.

Applied to medical care, the effect of a non-delegable duty of care is that the principal, commonly an NHS trust, must ensure that reasonable care is taken in the provision of medical care to patients.

The doctrine of a non-delegable duty of care is often contrasted with that of vicarious liability (the liability of an employer for the torts of its employees, or those in a relationship analogous to employment, which are sufficiently closely connected to the employment). Vicarious liability is an alternative means by which the law imposes strict liability, but under an entirely different rationale. Much has been said about the link between the two doctrines. For now, it is worth noting that arguments regarding the existence of a non-delegable duty typically come to the fore when a task is delegated to an independent contractor. As there can be no vicarious liability for the torts of an independent contractor (characterised by the Supreme Court in *Barclays Bank Plc v Various Claimants*[5] at paragraph 27 as someone carrying on business on his own account), a claimant will need to establish that the task delegated was one for which the principal owed

---

4 [2017] UKSC 60; [2018] A.C. 335

5 Cf footnote 1

a non-delegable duty, to make him the subject of a claim. The vigorous restatement by the Supreme Court in 2020 of this principle of vicarious liability means that arguments about non-delegable duties will remain an important route for claimants in establishing liability.

CHAPTER THREE

THE COMMON LAW NON-DELEGABLE DUTY IN WOODLAND

Arguments for the existence of a non-delegable duty of care to a patient typically contend that such a duty arises at common law, so I turn to common law non-delegable duties first.

Non-delegable duties had long been recognised as arising in the context of certain relationships, but in *Woodland v Swimming Teachers Association and ors*[6] the Supreme Court articulated a unifying theory to describe the circumstances in which they arise[7].

The case concerned a tragic event in which a 10-year-old school pupil (the claimant) suffered a severe brain injury during a swimming lesson after she got into difficulties in the water. The swimming lesson had been arranged by the claimant's school (run by the defendant local education authority) and provided by independent contractors, pursuant to a contract entered by the school. It took place during school hours, but off school premises, and formed part of the national curriculum. The claimant contended that the defendant local education authority owed her a non-delegable duty in respect of the

---

6 Cf footnote 2

7 This book is concerned only with the second (and main) category of non-delegable duties identified by Lord Sumption (see [6-7] of the judgment), not the first category (summarised as extra-hazardous operations).

swimming lessons. The Supreme Court accepted this contention, overturning the decision of the Court of Appeal.

Lord Sumption, giving the leading judgment, stated that the starting point for a non-delegable duty was a relationship between the two parties which gave rise to a positive duty on the part of the defendant to protect a particular class of persons against a particular class of risks (paragraph 7). Examples of relationships in which this duty arose included those between an employer and its employees, a hospital and its patients, and a school and its pupils.

After analysing a sweep of past cases on non-delegable duties, he set out the five defining features of a non-delegable duty at paragraph 23:

> *"…If the highway and hazard cases are put to one side, the remaining cases are characterised by the following defining features:*
>
> *(1) The claimant is a patient or a child, or for some other reason is especially vulnerable or dependent on the protection of the defendant against the risk of injury. Other examples are likely to be prisoners and residents in care homes.*
>
> *(2) There is an antecedent relationship between the claimant and the defendant, independent of the negligent act or omission itself, (i) which places the claimant in the actual custody, charge or care of the defendant, and (ii) from which it is possible to impute to the defendant the assumption of a positive duty to protect the claimant from harm, and not just a duty to refrain from conduct which will foreseeably damage the claimant. It is characteristic of such relationships that*

they involve an element of control over the claimant, which varies in intensity from one situation to another, but is clearly very substantial in the case of schoolchildren.

(3) *The claimant has no control over how the defendant chooses to perform those obligations, ie whether personally or through employees or through third parties.*

(4) *The defendant has delegated to a third party some function which is an integral part of the positive duty which he has assumed towards the claimant; and the third party is exercising, for the purpose of the function thus delegated to him, the defendant's custody or care of the claimant and the element of control that goes with it.*

(5) *The third party has been negligent not in some collateral respect but in the performance of the very function assumed by the defendant and delegated by the defendant to him."*

Imposition of a non-delegable duty also needs to be fair, just and reasonable (paragraph 25), although the Supreme Court in *Armes*[8] has clarified that this threshold is met if the five defining features are satisfied.

Lady Hale stated in a concurring judgment that Lord Sumption's five defining features should not be read as statute or treated as set in stone (paragraphs 28 and 38).

8 Cf footnote 4

Lord Sumption analysed the <u>*Woodland*</u> case in terms of the five defining features at paragraph 26:

> *"In my opinion, on the limited facts pleaded or admitted, the respondent education authority assumed a duty to ensure that the claimant's swimming lessons were carefully conducted and supervised, by whomever they might get to perform these functions. The claimant was entrusted to the school for certain essential purposes, which included teaching and supervision. The swimming lessons were an integral part of the school's teaching function. They did not occur on school premises, but they occurred in school hours in a place where the school chose to carry out this part of its functions. The teaching and the supervisory functions of the school, and the control of the child that went with them, were delegated by the school to Mrs Stopford and through her to Ms Burlinson, and probably to Ms Maxwell as well, to the extent necessary to enable them to give swimming lessons. The alleged negligence occurred in the course of the very functions which the school assumed an obligation to perform and delegated to its contractors. It must follow that if the latter were negligent in performing those functions and the child was injured as a result, the educational authority is in breach of duty."*

The existence of a non-delegable duty at common law therefore depends on a relationship independent of the alleged negligence which places the defendant in a position of having charge over the claimant.

It can be contrasted with the doctrine of vicarious liability in several ways. Whereas vicarious liability hinges upon the relationship between the defendant and the tortfeasor, a non-delegable duty hinges upon the relationship between the defendant and the claimant. A non-delegable duty is a form of direct liability, pursuant to which a defendant will be found to have breached its own personal duty to the claimant, but vicarious liability is imposed on the defendant without breach of duty on its part.

CHAPTER FOUR

COMMON LAW NON-DELEGABLE DUTIES IN MEDICAL CARE

The background to the non-delegable duty in the hospital-patient relationship

As above, Lord Sumption cites the relationship between a hospital and its patients as a paradigmatic example of one which gives rise to a non-delegable duty of care. The principle that this relationship gives rise to a non-delegable duty has long been established in English case law, although, until recently, all judicial dicta on the point were obiter.

I highlight a few of the pre-*Woodland* cases below:

In *Gold v Essex County Council*[9] Lord Greene MR in the Court of Appeal gave judgment in favour of a claimant hospital patient on the basis of what is recognisably a non-delegable duty. The point was obiter because the majority of the Court (Mackinnon and Goddard LJJ) found in her favour on the separate ground of vicarious liability. The claimant suffered injury due to the negligence of a radiographer employed by the defendant hospital, who failed to cover her face properly during treatment with Grenz rays. Lord Greene reasoned at p 301:

9 [1942] 2 K.B. 293 (CA)

> *"...In the former case [of a contractual relationship] there is, of course, a remedy in contract, while in the latter [case of a non-contractual relationship] the only remedy is in tort, but in each case the first task is to discover the extent of the obligation assumed by the person whom it is sought to make liable. Once this is discovered, it follows of necessity that the person accused of a breach of the obligation cannot escape liability because he has employed another person, whether a servant or agent, to discharge it on his behalf, and this is equally true whether or not the obligation involves the use of skill..."*

Similarly, in the cases of *Cassidy v Ministry of Health*[10] and *Roe v Minister of Health*[11], Denning LJ found that the defendant (responsible for the hospitals) owed a non-delegable duty to patients, but the majority of the Court of Appeal proceeded on the basis of a finding of vicarious liability.

For a long time thereafter the question of whether a hospital owed a non-delegable duty to its patients was not subject to judicial decision in England and Wales because hospital authorities did not challenge that they were responsible for the negligence of their clinical staff. But it is apparent from the following cases that hospitals were understood to owe such a duty:

In *X (Minors) v Bedfordshire County Council*[12] (a House of Lords case concerning private law causes of action for breach of statutory

---

10 [1951] 2 K.B. 343

11 [1954] 2 Q.B. 66

12 [1995] 2 A.C. 633

obligations, since overruled by Poole BC v GN[13]) Lord Browne-Wilkinson at p 740 cited the hospital as an example of an entity owing what we would call a non-delegable duty: *"The position can be illustrated by reference to the hospital cases. It is established that those conducting a hospital are under a direct duty of care to those admitted as patients to the hospital (I express no view as to the extent of that duty). They are liable for the negligent acts of a member of the hospital staff which constitute a breach of that duty, whether or not the member of the staff is himself in breach of a separate duty of care owed by him to the plaintiff…"*.

The Court of Appeal in A (A Child) v Ministry of Defence[14] (more about the case below) stated at paragraph 63: *"…It seems to me that there are strong arguments of policy for holding that a hospital which offers treatment to a patient accepts responsibility for the care with which that treatment is administered regardless of the status of the person employed or engaged…"*.

Similarly, the Court of Appeal in Farraj v King's Healthcare NHS Trust[15] (more about the case below) stated at paragraph 88:

> *"I am prepared to assume, without deciding, that the editors of Clerk & Lindsell are right and that English law has now reached the stage that the approach advocated by Lord Greene MR in Gold v Essex County Council [1942] 2 KB 293 and Denning LJ in Cassidy v Ministry of Health [1951] 2 KB 343 should be adopted. It is true that the extent to which a hospital owes a non-delegable duty to ensure that its patients*

13 [2019] UKSC 25; [2020] A.C. 780

14 [2004] EWCA Civ 641; [2005] Q.B. 183

15 [2009] EWCA Civ 1203; [2010] 1 W.L.R. 2139

> *are treated with due skill and care will depend on the facts of the particular case. But I shall assume that a hospital generally owes a non-delegable duty to its patients to ensure that they are treated with skill and care regardless of the employment status of the person who is treating them....*"

The theoretical basis for hospitals to owe their patients a non-delegable duty of care was developed in Australian case law, and broadly adopted by Lord Sumption in *Woodland* within his five defining features. I summarise two of those cases:

The Commonwealth v Introvigne,[16] a decision by the High Court of Australia, concerned a 15-year-old school child who was severely injured when larking around on school premises, an incident which would have been avoided if teaching staff had exercised reasonable care. The Commonwealth had established the school, but delegated the teaching to the State of New South Wales. The Court found that the Commonwealth, as the school authority, owed pupils a non-delegable duty of care, by analogy with the duty owed by a hospital to its patients (paragraph 28 of Mason J's judgment). Mason J reasoned at paragraph 30, "The immaturity and inexperience of the pupils and their propensity for mischief suggest that there should be a special responsibility on a school authority to care for their safety."

In *Kondis v State Transport Authority*,[17] another decision by the High Court of Australia, the claimant was injured at work through the negligence of a contractor hired by his employer. The High Court found the defendant liable on the basis of its non-delegable duty as employer. Mason J noted (paragraph 29) that a non-delegable duty

16 [1982] HCA 40; 150 CLR 258

17 [1984] HCA 61; 154 CLR 672

was also owed in the analogous relationships of a hospital and its patients, and a school authority and its pupils. His reasoning for the basis of the duty in these scenarios was as follows (paragraph 33):

> *"The element in the relationship between the parties which generates a special responsibility or duty to see that care is taken may be found in one or more of several circumstances. The hospital undertakes the care, supervision and control of patients who are in special need of care. The school authority undertakes like special responsibilities in relation to the children whom it accepts into its care... In these situations the special duty arises because the person on whom it is imposed has undertaken the care, supervision or control of the person or property of another or is so placed in relation to that person or his property as to assume a particular responsibility for his or its safety, in circumstances where the person affected might reasonably expect that due care will be exercised..."*

Lord Sumption's five defining features as applied to the hospital-patient relationship

I turn to consider the application of Lord Sumption's five defining features to the relationship between a hospital and its patients in more detail:

(1) "*The claimant is a patient or a child, or for some other reason is especially vulnerable or dependent on the protection of the defendant against the risk of injury.*"

It is assumed that hospital patients are particularly vulnerable or otherwise dependant on protection against the risk of injury. This stands to reason: a majority of hospital patients are there on account of a medical problem (be it physical or psychological); many will receive medical treatment for the same. A particular vulnerability does not need to be proven.

But it has been argued by academic Dr Christine Beuermann in her article *Do hospitals owe a so-called non-delegable duty to their patients?*[18] that the basis for regarding a patient as vulnerable or dependant is unclear. For example, a patient's medical condition may be more or less severe, thus rendering them more or less vulnerable in layman's terms, but this does not affect legal liability. She identifies the information deficit between a hospital and its patients, meaning the relative ignorance of medical matters shared by patients in contrast to medical staff, as the content of the "vulnerability" and "dependence" described by Lord Sumption under the first defining feature.

(2) *"There is an antecedent relationship between the claimant and the defendant, independent of the negligent act or omission itself, (i) which places the claimant in the actual custody, charge or care of the defendant, and (ii) from which it is possible to impute to the defendant the assumption of a positive duty to protect the claimant from harm, and not just a duty to refrain from conduct which will foreseeably damage the claimant. It is characteristic of such relationships that they involve an element of control over the claimant..."*

It is easy in the context of a hospital to see that there is a relationship between the hospital and a patient who has been admitted, and that this places the patient in the hospital's care. This is because the patient has attended with (in most cases) a medical problem, and is relying on the expertise of healthcare staff for advice or medical treatment.

---

18 Medical Law Review, Vol 26, No. 1, pp 1-26

The "element of control" over the patient is harder to identify. Dr Beuermann notes[19] that a hospital has physical control over the patient's use of its premises, although this is no different to any occupier-visitor relationship. It may also have some control over the patient's body, depending on how invasive a medical procedure is being carried out.

More fundamentally, the concept of a hospital having control over a patient is out of step with the modern emphasis on patient choice and informed consent. In the 2015 Supreme Court case of *Montgomery v Lanarkshire Health Board*[20] the law was changed regarding a doctor's duty to disclose to a patient information about the risks of treatment[21]. It is now settled that a doctor owes their patient a duty to take reasonable care to ensure that they are aware of any material risks involved in recommended treatment and of any reasonable alternative or variant treatments[22]. Save in exceptional circumstances (such as where treatment is very urgent, where the patient is unconscious or otherwise unable to consent, or where disclosure of information would be seriously detrimental) medical procedures will therefore be limited to what a patient has agreed to. In a similar vein, the NHS Constitution reflects the centrality of patient choice: it pledges to,

---

19 In her article at footnote 18

20 [2015] UKSC 11; [2015] AC 1430

21 It had been the case that the *Bolam* test also applied to informing a patient of the risks of treatment. In other words, a doctor was only found to have acted negligently if no responsible body of medical opinion would have failed to disclose the information.

22 Paragraph 87 of *Montgomery*

"enable you to participate fully in your own healthcare decisions and to support you in making choices".[23]

Dr Beuermann in her article *Do hospitals owe a so-called non-delegable duty to their patients?*[24] and Professor Paula Giliker in her article *"Non-delegable duties and institutional liability for the negligence of hospital staff: fair, just and reasonable?"*[25] highlight the conflict between the paternalistic assumption inherent in applying Lord Sumption's second defining feature to hospitals, and the modern focus on patient autonomy.

The imputation to a hospital of the assumption of a positive duty to protect a patient is an objective assumption of responsibility. Its inclusion in the second defining feature has been criticised by Professor Giliker in her article above for adding nothing to the test. In this context she cites Keith Stanton's criticisms of the assumption of responsibility concept, namely that it is an attractive way of summarising a result, but of limited use in reaching that result.[26]

(3) *"The claimant has no control over how the defendant chooses to perform those obligations, ie whether personally or through employees or through third parties."*

Hospital patients do not, in the circumstances of a normal NHS hospital, have control over which healthcare professional they see, and, crucially, the person's employment status. They also do not have

[23] Under "Patients and the public: your rights and the NHS pledges to you"

[24] See footnote 18

[25] Tottel's Journal of Professional Negligence, 33(2), 109-127

[26] The article at footnote 25, p 14.

control over the structure for providing care in a particular hospital: for example, whether certain services (such as radiology) are outsourced to private companies, and when a patient should be referred to a more specialist hospital. If patients are occasionally able to express a preference as to how or by whom their care is provided, this is almost always subject to confirmation from the hospital that this is possible.

(4) "*The defendant has delegated to a third party some function which is an integral part of the positive duty which he has assumed towards the claimant; and the third party is exercising, for the purpose of the function thus delegated to him, the defendant's custody or care of the claimant and the element of control that goes with it.*"

(5) "*The third party has been negligent not in some collateral respect but in the performance of the very function assumed by the defendant and delegated by the defendant to him.*"

The "integral" part of the hospital's duty to its patients and the hospital's care of and control over the patient (in the fourth defining feature) is likely to refer to the provision of actual medical services (such as healthcare advice, medical procedures etc.)

Negligence in a "collateral respect" (the fifth defining feature) is harder to define. Professor Giliker in her article above describes the term "collateral negligence" as notoriously vague.[27] For example, it is arguable either way whether the negligent failure to provide a suitable bed for an elderly inpatient – unconnected with the medical care he is receiving – would count as collateral negligence.

27 The article at footnote 25

Other case law addressing the common law non-delegable duty in medical care

The Supreme Court in *Woodland* aimed to be consistent with earlier case law which addressed the existence of a non-delegable duty in respect of medical care. Lord Sumption's description of the five defining features carefully avoided conflicting with the outcomes reached in earlier Court of Appeal decisions. Various decisions concerning medical care have followed *Woodland*, interpreting it for a range of healthcare scenarios. I turn now to summarising the important decisions regarding non-delegable duties in medical care, both before and after *Woodland*, highlighting the key principles relevant to determination of whether a non-delegable duty will arise. The cases concern medical care in the following settings, and I approach them in this order:

- hospitals;
- prisons and detention centres;
- dental surgeries;
- cancer screening programmes.

Cases addressing the non-delegable duty for medical care in hospitals

A (A Child) v Ministry of Defence [2004] EWCA Civ 641; [2004] 3 W.L.R. 469

The claimant was injured because of negligent obstetric care in a hospital in Germany. His father was a soldier employed by the first defendant, the Ministry of Defence ("MOD"), in Germany. The

MOD had a duty to arrange medical care for servicemen and their dependants, such as the claimant. At the material time it had subcontracted the provision of secondary care to hospitals in Germany, having run its own military hospitals in Germany in the past. The claimant argued that, once in Germany, the claimant's parents came under the protection of the MOD, and it owed them a non-delegable duty to provide reasonable medical treatment. This was rejected at first instance and by the Court of Appeal. Lord Sumption in *Woodland* noted that medical care was arranged by the MOD, but not provided by the MOD, and there was therefore no delegation of a function for which it had assumed responsibility (paragraph 24). He rejected Lord Phillips' reasoning at paragraph 43 of *A (A Child)*.

Farraj v King's Healthcare NHS Trust and another [2009] EWCA Civ 1203; [2010] 1 W.L.R. 2139

The claimants, who were carriers of a gene which caused a blood disorder, instructed the first defendant NHS trust to conduct DNA sampling of foetal tissue. The Trust contracted with a laboratory (the second defendant) which cleaned and cultured the sample, returned it to the first defendant, and negligently failed to inform it of concerns that the sample contained no foetal tissue. The Court of Appeal rejected the claimants' submission that the Trust owed them a non-delegable duty. They had not been admitted to the Trust's hospital for treatment, as required for a non-delegable duty to arise (paragraph 92). Had they been admitted, a non-delegable duty would have been owed.

In both cases there was no antecedent relationship between the claimant and the defendant independent of the negligent act. The defendant merely arranged, but did not provide, medical care.

Mabey v Kulkarni (2022, County Court, unreported)

The claimant received private medical treatment from Mr Kulkarni, an orthopaedic surgeon (the first defendant), at St Joseph's Hospital (the second defendant). He had no written contract with Mr Kulkarni, but had a contract with the hospital, which stated that he was liable to pay the hospital for any nursing care, but that the consultant was neither an employee nor an agent of the hospital and would invoice the claimant separately. Mr Kulkarni invoiced and corresponded with the claimant in the name of his company. The claimant alleged negligence in respect of specific outpatient appointments with Mr Kulkarni. He contended that St Joseph's Hospital owed a non-delegable duty of care in respect of the same, relying on the case of *Hughes v Rattan* (see below). The Judge rejected this submission, finding that the second and third defining features of a non-delegable duty were not present. The hospital had no contractual obligation to provide any service to the claimant and received no financial payment for the appointments (save for room rental payments). The claimant had complete control over who he saw.

Cases addressing the non-delegable duty for medical care of detainees

Morgan v Ministry of Justice [2010] EWHC 2248 (QB)

The claimants sued the Ministry of Justice ("MOJ") (the first defendant) in respect of the suicide of a young man in prison, allegedly due to the negligence of medical staff. They contended that a non-delegable duty was owed by the MOJ (the state department in charge of prisons) to the deceased prisoner to provide reasonable medical care at the prison. At the material time, the local Primary Care Trust ("PCT") was responsible for providing medical care under the statutory scheme; it had previously been the responsibility of HM

Prison Service. Supperstone J found, obiter, that no such non-delegable duty was owed by the MOJ. Following the transfer of healthcare to the PCT, the MOJ no longer provided healthcare services. Its duty to the deceased had been limited to a duty to provide access to healthcare services (paragraph 35).

Prisoners are a category of persons identified by Lord Sumption as likely to satisfy the first of the five defining features. If the defendant is responsible for detainees' imprisonment, and that includes responsibility for their medical care, a non-delegable duty will be owed.

Nyang v G4S Care and Justice Services Limited and ors
[2013] EWHC 3946 (QB)

The claimant received negligent medical treatment while detained in an immigration removal centre. The centre was operated entirely by the first defendant, G4S, pursuant to a contract with the Secretary of State for the Home Department. The relevant Detention Centre Rules required G4S to have a medical practitioner and healthcare team available for the detained persons. G4S conceded (paragraph 96) that it owed a non-delegable duty to detainees in respect of their medical care.

GB v Home Office [2015] EWHC 819 (QB)

As in *Nyang* above, the claimant contended that she had received negligent medical care while detained in an immigration removal centre. But she brought a claim against the Home Office, and not Serco, the private company which the Home Office had engaged to operate the centre. Coulson J, applying *Woodland*'s five defining features, found that the Home Office owed a non-delegable duty.

This is a puzzling decision: from the facts given, it appears that the Home Office delegated all its responsibility for the immigration centre to Serco. As such, and by analogy with the cases of *A (A Child)* and *Farraj*, it is unclear how there was an antecedent relationship (the second defining feature) between the claimant and the Home Office.

Razumas v Ministry of Justice [2018] EWHC 215 (QB); [2018] P.I.Q.R. P10

On facts similar to the case of *Morgan*, the claimant, then a prisoner, received negligent medical care at a time after, pursuant to a statutory regime change, responsibility for healthcare at the prison had been transferred from the MOJ to the local PCT. The MOJ accepted (paragraph 139) that it had owed a non-delegable duty in respect of medical care prior to the statutory change, at which time medical care had been the responsibility of the prison; it denied that it owed such a duty after the change. Accepting this argument, Cockerill J found that there was no non-delegable duty owed by the MOJ to provide reasonable medical care: the provision of healthcare was the duty of the PCT and its subcontractors (paragraph 153). Cockerill J reasoned as follows, rephrasing the *Woodland* test (emphasis mine):

> *"150. …**there is a nexus between the control of the claimant by the target and the purpose of that control/placing, and the care inherent in that relationship**. That facet can be easily seen in a hospital, as regards healthcare – a patient gives himself over to the hospital for the very purpose of healthcare. Or as Lord Sumption put it at [30] the claimant, as well as being in the target's care should*

> *be "receiving a service which is part of the institution's mainstream function". To similar effect is Baroness Hale's point at [40] and also [42] that the conundrum in the Woodland case resulted from "outsourcing of essential aspects of [public authorities'] functions".*
>
> *151. Here the reasoning breaks down in the current case: the reason for the prisoner being in the hands of the prison is not for, and does not comprehend, healthcare. Healthcare is not (at least since 2003) part of the prison institution's mainstream (or essential) function. It has not been outsourced by the Defendant…"*

Cases addressing the non-delegable duty for dental care

Hughes v Rattan [2022] EWCA Civ 107; [2022] 1 W.L.R. 1680

This is the first appellate decision of a superior court in England and Wales to find as its ratio that a non-delegable duty of care is owed in a medical care setting. I therefore consider it in some detail.

The claimant sued Dr Rattan, the owner of a dental practice (the "Practice"), for negligent NHS dental care. The care had been provided to the claimant by four dentists, one of whom was employed by the Practice, and the remainder of whom were self-employed. She contended that Dr Rattan owed her a non-delegable duty of care in respect of the treatment she had received.

All patients attending the Practice received a "Personal Dental Treatment Plan" form for each course of treatment. Dr Rattan's name was given next to "Provider's details". No other dentist was named on the form. The form stated: "The dentist named on this form is providing you with a course of treatment…".

NHS dental care at the Practice was provided pursuant to a lengthy (157-page) General Dental Services ("GDS") Contract between Dr Rattan and the PCT. Under the contract Dr Rattan agreed to carry out a specified amount of dental work (expressed in terms of "units of dental activity") per year. He was entitled to sub-contract this work, so long as certain conditions were met, including that the individual dentist was qualified, competent and adequately insured. Dr Rattan was paid directly by the PCT for the work.

The Practice's self-employed dentists had contracts with Dr Rattan which used the British Dental Association standard template contract. Importantly, the dentists agreed to carry insurance and to indemnify Dr Rattan for costs incurred due to breach of the contract; they were subject to strict restrictive covenants in the event of leaving the Practice. They had complete clinical control over the dental treatment provided to patients.

Dr Rattan paid the self-employed dentists 50% of the fees received from the PCT under the GDS contract. From the remaining 50% he paid the running costs of the Practice (for example, staff salaries).

The Court of Appeal, led by Lord Justice Bean, concluded that the first instance Judge (Heather Williams QC) had been "clearly right" (paragraph 68) to find that Dr Rattan owed a non-delegable duty, dismissing his appeal. Most of the disagreement focused on Lord Sumption's second defining feature: the need for an antecedent relationship, which placed the claimant in Dr Rattan's care. The Court of Appeal found that there was an antecedent relationship at the latest when the claimant signed the Personal Dental Treatment Plan. This placed the claimant in the care of Dr Rattan as owner of the practice, and involved an element of control (paragraph 71(2)), notwithstanding that the self-employed dentists had clinical control over treatment. As to the third defining feature, the claimant's ability to express a preference as to which dentist she saw did not alter the fact that Dr Rattan was in control of how the Practice performed its obligations.

The Court of Appeal considered the following facts to be significant (paragraphs 69 and 70):

- the wording of the Personal Dental Treatment Plan;
- that the contracts between Dr Rattan and the self-employed dentists used the term "patients of the practice";
- stringent restrictive covenants applied to the self-employed dentists.

The decision is thus a fact-specific application of Lord Sumption's five defining features in the context of a particular, albeit typical, dental surgery.

Of interest: regarding the application of the first defining feature ("The claimant is a patient or a child, or for some other reason is especially vulnerable or dependent..."), the Court of Appeal stated at paragraph 71(1): "*Whether it includes medical or dental patients who are not actually subjected to treatment, but merely advised in consultation, is a question for another case and another day.*"

The earlier County Court decisions of *Ramdhean v Agedo and another* (unreported) and *Breakingbury v Croad* (unreported) found that a non-delegable duty was owed by a dental practice or its owner on similar facts. In both cases:

- the practice or its owner had a contract with the PCT or local health board to carry out dental work, which permitted subcontracting;
- the relevant dentists at the practice were self-employed;
- the dentists were introduced to the claimants through the dental practices; and
- of the money paid by the PCT, the dentists received 50% or less.

Cases addressing the non-delegable duty for a cancer screening programme

Morrissey v Health Service Executive [2020] IESC 6; [2020] P.N.L.R. 17

The Supreme Court of Ireland has addressed the existence of a common law non-delegable duty in the case of a screening programme for cervical cancer. The defendant Health Service Executive ("HSE") is the entity in the Republic of Ireland responsible for the provision of health services. The CervicalCheck programme was established in 2008 by the National Cancer Screening Services Board ("NCSSB") and was run by the HSE (taking over from the NCSSB) from 2010. Independent laboratories were contracted to test and report on smear samples. The claimant's two cervical smear tests in 2009 and 2012 were incorrectly reported as negative due to the negligence of laboratory staff. The Supreme Court, by analogy with *Woodland*, found that the HSE owed a non-delegable duty to users of the

CervicalCheck programme, because it was responsible for the scheme and had not divested itself of responsibility for the same[28].

It is unclear whether this result would have been reached by an English court. It is questionable whether the claimant had an antecedent relationship with the HSE or whether, instead, the facts were analogous to the case of *Farraj v King's Healthcare NHS Trust*. Further, the Supreme Court of Ireland appears to have placed some reliance on the reasonable person's perception that the HSE was responsible for the programme (paragraph 13.26). The English courts have generally considered reasonable perception to be irrelevant[29].

Direct liability of a hospital for organisational failures

A hospital's duty of care to patients in the organisation of its resources is a distinct form of direct liability, to be distinguished from the unrelated doctrine of the non-delegable duty of care. Its only real similarity to the non-delegable duty principle is that it may form the basis for a claim against a hospital or health authority without the need for a negligent employee to be identified.

The Court of Appeal in *Wilsher v Essex Area Health Authority*[30] affirmed (obiter) the direct liability of a health authority for

28 It is unclear from the judgment how it might do this: see paragraphs 13.24 and 13.25.

29 See *A (A Child) v Ministry of Defence* at paragraph 61 and the High Court decision in *Hughes v Rattan* [2021] EWHC 2032 at paragraph 113.

30 [1987] Q.B. 730. The decision was overturned by the House of Lords on unrelated grounds.

organisational failures at p 778 and p 775 (per Browne-Wilkinson VC and Glidewell LJ respectively):

> *"In my judgment, a health authority which so conducts its hospital that it fails to provide doctors of sufficient skill and experience to give the treatment offered at the hospital may be directly liable in negligence to the patient... I can see no reason why, in principle, the health authority should not be so liable if its organisation is at fault."*

> *"Firstly, I agree with the Vice-Chancellor that there seems to be no reason in principle why, in a suitable case different on its facts from this, a hospital management committee should not be held directly liable in negligence for failing to provide sufficient qualified and competent medical staff."*

CHAPTER FIVE

EXAMPLE SCENARIOS

Lawyers encounter a huge range of factual scenarios in healthcare claims. I set out below example scenarios and comments on each, including, where appropriate, lines of inquiry and arguments in favour of and against the existence of a common law non-delegable duty of care.

Scenario 1

Claimant A attends the emergency department of a hospital after falling and injuring his hand. He is booked into the hospital by a receptionist, and then seen by a triage nurse, who takes a note of his symptoms, and asks him to take a seat. He is then seen by an emergency department doctor, who, unknown to Claimant A, is an independent contractor and not employed by the NHS Trust which runs the hospital. The doctor examines his hand and asks him about the mechanism of injury and his symptoms. He then discharges Claimant A, with instructions to attend his GP after seven days if symptoms persist. His fracture goes undiagnosed. According to Claimant A's expert evidence, the doctor fails to arrange an x-ray and referral to the orthopaedic surgeon, which would have resulted in prompt diagnosis and surgical treatment that day.

Comment

With Claimant A attending a physical hospital, run by a particular NHS trust, he is very likely to be owed a non-delegable duty by medical professionals working at that hospital (per *Woodland* et al). If everyone whom Claimant A is seen by at the hospital is employed by a particular independent company rather than by the NHS Trust (very unlikely), there would be an argument that there is no antecedent relationship between Claimant A and the NHS Trust. The counter argument to this would be that, analogous to the dental negligence cases in chapter 4, Claimant A does not need to receive medical care from the NHS Trust's employees for the second defining feature to be satisfied: it is enough for the NHS Trust to have "the care, supervision and control" of Claimant A as its patient. Claimant A should also consider whether the NHS Trust is vicariously liable (likely to be the case, but beyond the scope of this book).

Scenario 2

Claimant B attends her GP complaining of chest pain of recent onset and a permanent cough. She is a lifelong smoker. Her GP makes an urgent referral to the respiratory department of an NHS Trust, for her to have an appointment with a chest physician. She is seen by a chest physician at the hospital (managed by the NHS Trust) within seven days, and a chest x-ray is performed. The x-ray film is then sent off to a private company to be interpreted by a radiologist, pursuant to a contract between the NHS Trust and that company. The radiologist who considers the film negligently completes a report stating that no cancer is visible, because of a mix-up with the x-ray film of a different patient. The NHS Trust's chest physician is reassured by the report and gives X a differential diagnosis of COPD, for which she starts treatment. Claimant B's cancer is not diagnosed until a long time later.

Comment

The facts are the inverse of those in *Farraj v King's Healthcare NHS Trust*, in which no non-delegable duty was owed because the claimants were never admitted to the hospital as patients, but merely instructed the defendant NHS Trust to analyse a tissue sample. Here, Claimant B self-evidently was admitted to the hospital as a patient under the care of the respiratory department, and had no control over the NHS Trust's decision to engage an independent company to interpret x-rays. The interpretation of the chest x-ray will be regarded as an integral part of the NHS Trust's duty towards him, in the performance of which the independent company was negligent. Thus *Woodland*'s five defining features will be met. Any argument is likely to centre around whether Claimant B was a patient of the hospital, but on the facts above it is hard to anticipate any serious dispute. The NHS Trust should consider making a Part 20 claim for an indemnity against the company, or subsequently bringing contribution proceedings against the company under the Civil Liability (Contribution) Act 1978.

Scenario 3

Claimant C is referred by her GP to the gynaecology department of an NHS hospital, due to suffering from stress and urge incontinence and defecatory dysfunction. Over the course of 12 months, she attends multiple appointments with gynaecologists at the hospital, at which a range of investigations are carried out. It is decided that Claimant C should undergo urodynamic studies, to take place at separate premises where there is capacity for this in the next fortnight. (The NHS hospital's equipment for urodynamic studies is booked for back-to-back use by patients for the next three months.) The separate premises is run by an independent company which provides a full range of gynaecology services, including employing a team of gynaecologists.

The company receives Claimant C's medical records, a letter from her gynaecologist at the NHS hospital, and arranges for her to have the urodynamic studies and a follow-up appointment with a gynaecologist. At the end the company's gynaecologist writes a report to the NHS Trust, and Claimant C's involvement with the company ceases. It turns out that the urodynamic studies were not performed competently, resulting in Claimant C's condition going undiagnosed.

Comment

The parties will want to see the letters which have passed between the NHS Trust and the independent company, and any contract between the two. It will be instructive to learn how the NHS Trust describes the role of the company: whether carrying out urodynamic studies "for the Trust's patient" or receiving a referral to carry out said studies and advise Claimant C of the results. On the face of it, *Woodland*'s five defining features appear to be satisfied. Claimant C can point to the fact that she had no choice in having urodynamic studies carried out by a different treatment provider. She can also argue that the NHS Trust remained in overall charge of her gynaecological care, such that she was always their patient. The NHS Trust's counter argument will be that Claimant C was referred out of the Trust for a particular procedure (which the hospital had the facilities to perform) and that she ceased to be their patient in respect of that care.

Scenario 4

The facts are the same as in scenario 3, save that Claimant D is referred by the NHS Trust to (a) a different NHS Trust for (b) all of her gynaecological care, because (c) the primary NHS Trust does not have capacity, and (d) X agrees to the referral.

Comment

With all of Claimant D's care transferred to a different NHS Trust, she is now their patient and cannot be described as being in the "custody, charge or care" of the first NHS Trust. If Claimant D wants to fix the first NHS Trust with liability (it is hard to see what benefit this would offer her) she may argue that the first NHS Trust delegated the function of providing her healthcare to the second Trust. But in circumstances that the second NHS Trust has permanently taken over her care, the first NHS Trust can say (indisputably) that their care of her ceased when she was transferred over.

Scenario 5

Claimant E is admitted to an NHS hospital as an inpatient suffering from severe symptoms of Crohn's disease (anal fistulas, abscesses, and acute abdominal pain). The NHS Trust's consultant colorectal surgeon recommends a reversible loop ileostomy to reduce stress on the anal canal, which Claimant E agrees to. Unfortunately neither she nor any of her colleagues have capacity to carry out the operation for several months because of more urgent surgeries taking priority. Claimant E is therefore given the opportunity of paying for the surgery to be performed privately, which he takes up. Unusually, the private surgeon and support staff (all employed by a private company) carry out the operation at the NHS hospital, rather than requiring Claimant E to travel, but they do so outside NHS hours. The surgeon performs the procedure without sufficient care and Claimant E suffers a small bowel obstruction as a result. He remains an inpatient at the NHS hospital and is treated for the small bowel obstruction (in addition to the Crohn's disease) by the NHS Trust's staff. Operation aftercare is also provided by the NHS Trust.

Comment

The parties will want to look at the terms of the contract between Claimant E and the private company (or private surgeon). They will also want to look at the terms of any contract between the NHS Trust and the private company (or private surgeon), bearing in mind the use of the hospital's premises. Claimant E will argue, in favour of the existence of a non-delegable duty by the NHS Trust, that he never ceased to be their patient. But Claimant E chose to engage a private surgeon, and the NHS Trust therefore has a very strong argument that the third of *Woodland*'s defining features (that the patient had no control over how the defendant performed its obligations) is not satisfied. It also has a strong argument that the fourth defining feature is not satisfied: the NHS Trust did not delegate the surgery to the private company, but Claimant E opted for private care.

Scenario 6

Claimant F attends an appointment with his named GP and explains that he wishes to have a vasectomy, as he has decided his family is complete. His GP (who is a partner at the surgery) discusses this with him and is satisfied that he has thought the decision through. None of the GPs at the surgery are trained to perform vasectomies (the one GP who used to carry them out has recently retired), so his GP refers Claimant F to a sexual health clinic for the procedure. The clinic is run by a private company. A urologist at the clinic carries out the procedure on Claimant F. He develops severe epididymitis, requiring extensive treatment, a complication of the procedure. His evidence is that he was not advised of the risk of this complication, and would not have gone ahead with the procedure if he had been.

Comment

A vasectomy is a procedure which may be carried out by a GP, at surgery premises. Claimant F's vasectomy would have been performed at his surgery if any of the GPs had been appropriately trained. Claimant F may therefore argue (in favour of a non-delegable duty of care) that the GP surgery has delegated part of its duty of providing healthcare to the private clinic, and Claimant F has had no control over this delegation. The GP surgery's counter argument is that a vasectomy falls outside the mainstream functions of a GP surgery, and in referring him to the private clinic ceased to have any responsibility for the vasectomy procedure. The NHS contract with the sexual health clinic pursuant to which the procedure was carried out may be relevant and should be obtained.

<u>Scenario 7</u>

Claimant G receives dental treatment over a number of years from dentists at a particular dental practice. One day she reports pain in multiple teeth, and it transpires that she is suffering from advanced gum disease, and will need them to be extracted. The disease is too advanced for conservative treatments to be effective. Her expert evidence is that the dentists at her dental practice gave overly optimistic readings for her basic periodontal examination (BPE) and failed to recognise the symptoms of gum disease, and advise her of the same. All the dentists are self-employed and are not partners of the practice. Claimant G wishes to bring a claim against the practice itself. Claimant G's personal dental treatment plan lists her named dentist (<u>not</u> the owner of the practice) as the "provider". Contracts between the practice and the self-employed dentists specify that patients are patients of the particular treating dentists and <u>not</u> patients of the practice (different to the case of <u>*Hughes v Rattan*</u>). On the other hand, the dentists are subject to restrictive covenants, use the practice's premises, have access to its equipment, and receive 50% of the money paid by the integrated care board (with which the practice has a general dental services contract) for units of dental activity.

Comment

The parties will want to see all of Claimant G's dental records, and contracts between the practice and the self-employed dentists. The practice in this case has taken steps to circumvent the decision in *Hughes v Rattan* in favour of a non-delegable duty of care: in particular the consistent description of patients as patients of treating dentists and not of the practice. The facts are otherwise the same as in *Hughes v Rattan*. Claimant G can argue in support of a non-delegable duty that, contrary to what is written down, the practice is in all respects providing a centralised service – introducing patients to dentists, providing premises and (if necessary) equipment, being privy to the contract with the integrated care board, and receiving 50% of the money received. Claimant G will also rely on the fact that dentists are subject to restrictive covenants in the event that they leave the practice. As such, Claimant G can argue that she was, as a matter of fact, a patient of the practice, with whom she had a relationship antecedent to that with the individual dentists. The practice's counter argument to this will be that the official documents do not describe patients of the practice (differentiating the case from *Hughes v Rattan*), and that (advancing similar arguments to the defendant in that case) there is no antecedent relationship between Claimant G and the practice. The practice can also argue that advice is in a different category to treatment (alluded to at paragraph 71(1) of *Hughes v Rattan*), and should not be subject to a non-delegable duty.

Scenario 8

Claimant H is detained in an immigration removal centre run by Serco. Medical care is provided by a GP surgery, which Serco has contracted with to provide primary medical care. Claimant H receives negligent medical care from a GP at the surgery, who fails to refer him for an urgent appointment with a psychiatrist. As a result Claimant H commits an act of self-harm, and suffers life-changing injuries.

Comment

Pursuant to the Detention Centre Rules 2001 a detention centre is required to have a health care team which includes a medical practitioner (a trained GP). Healthcare in this case was therefore the responsibility of Serco, which ran the immigration removal centre on behalf of the Home Office. Based on the current statutory regime, and following the reasoning in the case of *GB v Home Office*, Serco will owe a non-delegable duty of care, pursuant to *Woodland*, to detainees in respect of healthcare. Should the statutory regime change, and healthcare become the responsibility – say – of the integrated care board in that geographical area, the organisation running the detention centre can argue that its non-delegable duty is limited to providing access to healthcare (analogous to the position in *Razumas v MOJ*).

Scenario 9

Claimant I is a vulnerable elderly woman in the advanced stages of Alzheimer's dementia. She is admitted to the geriatric ward of an NHS hospital as an inpatient after suffering from dizziness and confusion. If her physical condition improves, it is anticipated that she will need to be discharged to a care home, rather than her home address (her husband has been increasingly struggling to look after her). The NHS Trust responsible for the hospital has contracted with an independent company to provide cleaning services on inpatient wards. The company is advised to take particular care always to leave the floor of the hospital's geriatric wards in a dry and clean state, because of the presence of vulnerable and incapacitous patients. A cleaner employed by the company leaves the floor between Claimant I's bed and the toilet in a wet state, and Claimant I slips on it, breaking her hip.

Comment

The parties will want to see the contract between the NHS trust and the cleaning company, in addition to Claimant I's medical records. Claimant I will argue that the Trust's duty towards her to provide medical care extends to providing overnight care in respect of her basic needs (such as accessing the toilet). This is an integral part of the Trust's duty to her, given her vulnerability due to advanced dementia. As an alternative to a non-delegable duty, Claimant I should consider whether any of the Trust's nursing staff ought to have noticed the wet floor and negligently failure to ensure that Claimant I made it to the toilet without incident. The Trust will argue that cleaning services are a paradigm example of something collateral to its duty of care, which is <u>not</u> an integral part of its duty. It is entitled to delegate the task, without retaining legal responsibility.

<u>Scenario 10</u>

Claimant J is a young child suffering from symptoms of fever, headache and loss of appetite on a bank holiday. Her mother rings the GP surgery, and receives an answer machine message advising patients to call NHS 111 for medical support, and 999 in cases of emergency. She calls NHS 111, and is directed to an out-of-hours centre, run by an independent company. She attends the out-of-hours centre with X, and is seen by a nurse, who discharges Claimant J and advises her mother to attend the GP surgery if her symptoms persist for a further five days. Claimant J's expert evidence is that the nurse gave the wrong safety netting advice, and should have told Claimant J's mother to take her to hospital if her symptoms persist for 24 hours. Claimant J has undiagnosed meningitis, and suffers severe brain damage.

Comment

Claimant J will not be able to establish a non-delegable duty by either the GP surgery or NHS 111, as neither organisation admitted her as a patient. But she has very strong argument that the company running the out-of-hours centre owed her a non-delegable duty once she was booked in as a patient.

CHAPTER SIX

STATUTORY NON-DELEGABLE DUTIES

A non-delegable duty may also arise pursuant to a statutory provision. The existence of a statutorily derived non-delegable duty is less commonly argued in medical negligence cases, given the strong arguments in favour of a common law non-delegable duty in a range of scenarios, as discussed above. Nonetheless it has been argued, and will no doubt be the subject of further case law in future.

A statutory non-delegable duty can be likened to a contractual provision under which one of the parties agrees to achieve a particular outcome. The party may delegate the task which is the subject of the provision, but it remains liable if, for whatever reason, the outcome promised in the contract is not achieved. Similar to claims for breach of contract, all will depend on the wording of the statutory provision as to the existence and content of the non-delegable duty.

The Supreme Court decision of *Armes v Nottinghamshire County Council*[31] is the leading case on non-delegable duties arising pursuant to statute. The claimant, a former foster child, appealed against the dismissal of her claim against the defendant local authority for the physical and sexual abuse she had suffered at the hands of her foster parents. It was agreed that the local authority had acted reasonably in the selection and supervision of the foster parents. The claimant

31 [2017] UKSC 60; [2018] A.C. 355

contended that (a) the local authority owed a non-delegable duty to ensure that reasonable care was taken for the safety of children in care, and (b) the local authority was vicariously liable for torts committed by foster carers against children in care. The Supreme Court allowed her appeal in respect of vicarious liability, but rejected her contention of a non-delegable duty of care.

Lord Reed, giving the Court's judgment, characterised the non-delegable duty point as follows (paragraph 37):

> *"The critical question, in deciding whether the local authority were in breach of a non-delegable duty in the present case, is whether the function of providing the child with day-to-day care, in the course of which the abuse occurred, was one which the local authority were themselves under a duty to perform with care for the safety of the child, or was one which they were merely bound to arrange to have performed, subject to a duty to take care in making and supervising those arrangements."*

He noted that the effect of the non-delegable duty asserted by the claimant would be extremely far-reaching, including that the local authority would act as insurer for torts committed by the child's family members, if placed with them pursuant to a care order (paragraph 45). He turned to the statutory provision which set out the local authority's duty in respect of accommodation and maintenance, section 21 of the Child Care Act 1980 (emphasis mine):

> *"(1) A local authority* ***shall discharge their duty*** *to provide accommodation and maintenance for a child in their care in such one of the following ways as they think fit, namely— (a) by boarding him out on such terms as to payment by the authority and otherwise as the authority may, subject to the*

> *provisions of this Act and regulations thereunder, determine; or (b) by maintaining him in a community home … or (c) by maintaining him in a voluntary home (other than a community home) …or by making such other arrangements as seem appropriate to the local authority…"*

He reasoned that the word "discharge" in section 21 implied that placement of the child constituted the performance of the local authority's duty (paragraph 47), in addition to compliance with the specific duties imposed on the local authority pursuant to regulations enacted under section 22 (paragraph 48). The duty was (paragraph 47), *"not to perform the function in the course of which the claimant was abused (namely, the provision of daily care), but rather to arrange for, and then monitor, its performance"*.

The decision in *Armes* was followed on very similar facts in the case of *SKX v Manchester City Council.*[32] The claimant suffered sexual abuse in a children's home in which he had been placed by the local authority under section 21(1) of the Child Care Act 1980 (see above). As per the case of *Armes*, Cavanagh J found that it was clear from the language of the provision that the local authority's duty was limited to arranging the placement (paragraph 92).

I summarise a selection of other cases which address whether a non-delegable duty is owed on the basis of a statutory or contractual provision:

- *Myton v Woods* [1980] C.L.Y. 861 (CA)

  The defendant education authority arranged for a taxi firm to transport two disabled children (one of whom was the

32 [2021] EWHC 782 (QB); [2021] 4 W.L.R. 56

claimant) to school each day. It did so pursuant to section 55 of the Education Act 1944 which required it to "make such arrangements for the provision of transport as they consider necessary... for the purpose of facilitating the attendance of pupils at schools... free of charge." The defendant instructed the taxi company as to where to pick up and set down the children. Instead the taxi driver negligently dropped the children on the opposite side of a busy main road. The claimant was severely injured crossing the road. The defendant was found not to owe a non-delegable duty in respect of the negligence of the taxi company (an independent contractor).

- *Rivers v Cutting* [1982] 1 W.L.R. 1146 (CA)

A police constable (employed by the defendant) arranged for the claimant's car to be removed by a garage. The car was damaged by an employee of the garage. He exercised powers under regulation 4 of the Removal and Disposal of Vehicles Regulations 1968, which stated, "*...a constable may remove or arrange for the removal of the vehicle...*". The claimant contended for what would now be described as a non-delegable duty of care, namely, to ensure that the vehicle was removed with reasonable care. The Court of Appeal found, rejecting the claimant's argument, that there were two distinct powers available to the constable; if exercising the power to arrange for removal, the duty was discharged by the exercise of reasonable care in selecting a garage.

- *Rogers v Night Riders* [1983] R.T.R. 324 (CA)

  The defendant firm operated a minicab service. They told the claimant's mother that a cab would be on its way. The claimant was injured because the car, which was driven by an independent contractor, was not fit for purpose. The Court found that the firm had held itself out to the general public as a minicab firm and undertook to provide the claimant with a minicab for her journey. Its duty, whether expressed in contract or tort, to take reasonable care to ensure that the car provided was reasonably fit for purpose, could not be delegated, in light of the information given to the claimant's mother.

- *Wong Mee Wan v Kwan Kin Travel Services Ltd* [1996] 1 W.L.R. 38 (Privy Council)

  The claimant's daughter bought a package tour of part of China from the first defendant travel company. She was killed in a speedboat crash due to the negligence of an independent contractor. The tour brochure, which contained the terms of the contract, set out the detailed itinerary planned for the tour. It made no reference to the first defendant arranging – as opposed to providing – the services. The Privy Council, allowing the claimant's appeal, found that the first defendant was obliged to provide the services with reasonable skill and care, even if it engaged the services of other companies.

It is worth noting that in many cases – such as those involving detention centres above – arguments have centred around whether a non-delegable duty arises at common law, notwithstanding a significant statutory backdrop. The existence of a statutory backdrop does not prevent a non-delegable duty arising at common law, so long as it is not ruled out by the statute. It is therefore important to consider, if the statute does not give rise to a non-delegable duty, whether such a duty may nonetheless arise at common law, as a result of the statutory arrangements. Cockerill J said this about the relevance of the statutory arrangements to determining the existence of a common law non-delegable duty at paragraph 157 of *Razumas*:

> *"Nor do I consider that there is any difficulty in the fact that the position as to duty has changed since the change in legislative provision. In the context of the flexibility of the common law principles and the authorities which indicate the complementary nature of the relationship between statute and common law there is nothing difficult or surprising in the position as to duty changing with such a major change in legislative arrangements. Nor is there any problem caused by the fact that the duty itself is not one set out in statute; that would be an artificial distinction and one which would sap flexibility from the common law."*

CHAPTER SEVEN

STATUTORY NON-DELEGABLE DUTIES IN MEDICAL CARE

I cite in chapter 8 some of the legislation which currently governs the provision of NHS healthcare in the UK. Any finding of a non-delegable duty of care arising from statute would have a very great impact on the liability of public sector bodies for medical negligence claims. No such duty has yet been accepted by the English courts in the context of extending liability.

In the case of *Razzel v Snowball*[33] the Court of Appeal was required to interpret section 3(1)(c) of the then NHS Act 1946, which stated, "it shall be the duty of the Minister [of Health] to provide throughout England and Wales... (c) the services of specialists whether at a hospital...". The defendant surgeon was engaged to work at a hospital pursuant to the same subsection. The Court of Appeal accepted that the claim against him was statute barred under section 21(1) of the Limitation Act 1939, on the basis that he was performing the duty of the Minister, and therefore came within the terms of that subsection. The Court of Appeal interpreted section 3(1) of the NHS Act 1946 to mean that the Minister's duty was to provide the necessary services, not merely to appoint competent specialists.

33 [1954] 1 W.L.R. 1382

In *Hopkins v Akramy*,[34] a 2020 High Court case, the claimant contended that a primary care trust (PCT) (for whose liabilities the NHS Commissioning Board was responsible) owed a non-delegable duty to recipients of primary medical services in its area on the basis of section 83(1) of the NHS Act 2006 (in its 2008 form). The contention was rejected. It does not appear that the above case of *Razzel* – in which the wording of the provision was similar but slightly different – was cited. The claimant had sustained severe brain injuries on account of (allegedly) negligent medical care provided to her in 2008 at an NHS out-of-hours clinic run by a private company. The company was uninsured and the nurse who saw the claimant had limited insurance cover. The care was provided pursuant to a contract between the PCT and the company, requiring the latter to provide out-of-hours primary medical services in South Birmingham. The PCT's duty in respect of primary medical services was set out in section 83(1) of the NHS Act 2006, on which the claimant relied as the basis of a non-delegable duty (emphases mine):

> *"83 Primary medical services*
>
> *(1) **Each Primary Care Trust must**, to the extent that it considers necessary to meet all reasonable requirements, exercise its powers so as to **provide primary medical services** within its area, **or secure their provision** within its area.*
>
> *(2) A Primary Care Trust may (in addition to any other power conferred on it)–*

[34] [2020] EWHC 3445 (QB); [2021] Q.B. 564

> *(a) provide primary medical services itself (whether within or outside its area),*
>
> *(b) make such arrangements for their provision (whether within or outside its area) as it considers appropriate, and may in particular make contractual arrangements with any person…"*

HHJ Melissa Clarke, sitting as a High Court judge, found (self-evidently) that the PCT's duty at section 83(1) could be discharged either by providing primary medical services, or by securing their provision. However, she went on to find that a duty to "secure [the] provision [of]" was equivalent to a duty to arrange. The duty could therefore be discharged by contracting with a third party, and was not non-delegable. In her view the statute ruled out the existence of a non-delegable duty, such that there was no need for her to consider whether such a duty arose at common law.

The author is not aware of any other recent case in which the existence of a statutory non-delegable duty in respect of healthcare has been argued.

CHAPTER EIGHT

NHS LEGISLATION, OUTSOURCING AND INSURANCE ARRANGEMENTS

This chapter will look briefly at the legislation governing provision of NHS healthcare (relevant to arguments in support of a statutory non-delegable duty) and then at indemnity cover for NHS and private healthcare (concerns about which are often the backdrop to arguments about non-delegable duties).

A brief history

The NHS has over the course of its history been subject to multiple waves of restructuring, which have been enacted by legislation. A detailed analysis of the set-up of the NHS, and its history, is beyond the scope of this book. Selected changes to the statutory framework of the NHS, which are of particular relevance to non-delegable duties, will be considered only. This chapter is limited to the organisation of the NHS in England.

An internal market was introduced to the NHS by the NHS and Community Care Act 1990. This Act split the roles of purchasing and providing healthcare between different health service bodies (see section 4). NHS contracts thereby assumed importance. The Act established NHS Trusts (section 5), which were intended to be quasi-autonomous corporate bodies contracted to provide healthcare services.

Primary Care Trusts were established in 2000 and abolished by the Health and Social Care Act 2012. NHS Foundation Trusts – which it had initially been planned would entirely replace NHS Trusts[35] – were established by the Health and Social Care (Community Health and Standards) Act 2003.

New Labour's NHS Plan 2000 sought to increase the competitiveness of the NHS's internal market by opening up competition to private healthcare providers. Alternative Provider Medical Services ("APMS") contracts for primary care services, which could be entered with private entities, were introduced several years later.

The NHS Constitution was established by the Health Act 2009. Health service bodies (such as NHS Trusts and NHS Foundation Trusts) have since been required to have regard to the Constitution in performing their health service functions (section 2).

The seven key principles of the NHS Constitution at the time of writing are as follows:

> *"1. The NHS provides a comprehensive service, available to all.*

35 There are still many NHS Trusts without foundation status and legislation (section 179 of the Health and Social Care Act 2012) to abolish all NHS Trusts was repealed by the Health and Care Act 2022.

2. *Access to NHS services is based on clinical need, not on an individual's ability to pay.*

3. *The NHS aspires to the highest standards of excellence and professionalism.*

4. *The patient will be at the heart of everything the NHS does.*

5. *The NHS works across organisational boundaries.*

6. *The NHS is committed to providing best value for taxpayers' money.*

7. *The NHS is accountable to the public, communities and patients that it serves."*

The Health and Social Care Act 2012 (the "HSCA") was a radical attempt to open up the NHS internal market to external competition. It established clinical commissioning groups ("CCGs"), which were based on the number of patients of GP members of the CCG[36], to commission care, and abolished area-based Primary Care Trusts. Under the legislation a CCG "must arrange for the provision of the following to such extent as it considers necessary to meet the reasonable requirements of the persons for whom it has responsibility... (c) medical, dental, ophthalmic, nursing and ambulance services...[37]". The CCG took over a duty on the Secretary of State for Health to "provide" the same services[38]. The Act also

36 Section 3(1A) of the NHS Act 2006, before amendment in 2022.

37 Section 3(1) of the NHS Act 2006, before amendment in 2022.

38 Section 3(1) of the NHS Act 2006, before amendment in 2012.

established the NHS Commissioning Board ("NHSCB"), known as NHS England, which shared with the Secretary of State for Health the duty under section 1(1) of the NHS Act 2006 to "continue the promotion in England of a comprehensive health service...[39]" The NHSCB was responsible for commissioning most primary care services: section 83(1) of the NHS Act 2006 stated, "The Board must, to the extent that it considers necessary to meet all reasonable requirements, exercise its powers so as to secure the provision of primary medical services throughout England." In the years following enactment of the HSCA outsourcing of NHS-funded care to private healthcare providers increased dramatically.

The most recent reorganisation of the NHS in England was by the Health and Care Act 2022 (the "HCA"). The Act can be seen as an attempt to reverse the trend towards much greater competition for NHS contracts brought in by the HSCA.[40] CCGs were abolished and replaced by integrated care boards ("ICBs"), to form part of new integrated care systems ("ICSs"). The function of an ICB is to arrange for the provision of services, taking the place of CCGs in the legislative framework.[41] ICSs comprise ICBs and integrated care partnerships ("ICPs"); the latter contain representatives of ICBs and local authorities and each ICP is required to prepare a strategy ("an integrated care strategy") as to how needs in its area are to be met.[42] ICSs have been described as partnerships that bring providers and

---

39 Before amendment in 2022.

40 Section 75 of the HSCA, and regulations made thereunder, required almost all NHS contracts to be put out to competitive tender. Section 75 HSCA was repealed by the HCA.

41 Sections 1I and 3(1) of the NHS Act 2006

42 Section 26 HCA.

commissioners of NHS services together with local partners to plan healthcare services for the local population.[43]

The emphasis of the HCA is thus on collaboration between different organisations through ICSs to provide integrated care, rather than on competition for contracts. But it is worth noting that whatever the intended emphasis, as was the case with CCGs, the function of ICBs is to enter contracts with particular providers for the provision of healthcare services.

The HCA also renamed the NHSCB NHS England.[44]

Current legislation

Extracts

The NHS Act 2006:

Section 1: Secretary of State's duty to promote comprehensive health service

> *"(1) The Secretary of State must continue the promotion in England of a comprehensive health service designed to secure improvement-*
>
> > *(a) in the physical and mental health of the people in England, and*

---

43 P 74 of Mason and McCall-Smith's *Law and Medical Ethics*, 12th edition

44 Section 1(1) HCA and section 1H of the NHS Act 2006.

> *(b) in the prevention, diagnosis and treatment of physical and mental illness…"*

Section 1H: NHS England and its general functions

> *"…(2) NHS England is subject to the duty under section 1(1) concurrently with the Secretary of State except in relation to that part of the health service that is provided in pursuance of the public health functions of the Secretary of State or local authorities…"*

Section 1I: General functions of integrated care boards

> *"An integrated care board established under Chapter A3 of Part 2 has the function of arranging for the provision of services for the purposes of the health service in England in accordance with this Act."*

Section 3: Duties of integrated care boards as to commissioning certain health services

> *"(1) An integrated care board must arrange for the provision of the following to such extent as it considers necessary to meet the reasonable requirements of the people for whom it has responsibility—*
>
> *(a) hospital accommodation…*
>
> *(c) medical services other than primary medical services (for primary medical services, see Part 4),*
>
> *(d) dental services other than primary dental services (for primary dental services, see Part 5),*

(e) ophthalmic services other than primary ophthalmic services (for primary ophthalmic services, see Part 6),

(f) nursing and ambulance services…

(3) The duty imposed on an integrated care board by subsection (1) to arrange for the provision of services or facilities does not apply to the extent that—

(a) NHS England has a duty to arrange for their provision…"

Section 83: Primary medical services

"(1) The Board must, to the extent that it considers necessary to meet all reasonable requirements, exercise its powers so as to secure the provision of primary medical services throughout England.

(2) The Board may (in addition to any other power conferred on it) make such arrangements for the provision of primary medical services as it considers appropriate; and it may, in particular, make contractual arrangements with any person…"

Section 83: General power [not yet in force]

"(1) An integrated care board may make such arrangements for the provision of primary medical services as it considers appropriate for the purpose of discharging its functions under section 82B (and may, in particular, make contractual arrangements with any person).

(2) NHS England may make such arrangements for the provision of primary medical services as it considers appropriate for the purpose of discharging any functions under section 3B(1) (and may, in particular, make contractual arrangements with any person)…"

Section 84: General medical services contracts: introductory

"(1) The Board may enter into a contract under which primary medical services are provided in accordance with the following provisions of this Part.

(2) A contract under this section is called in this Act a "general medical services contract"…"

Section 84: General medical services contracts: introductory [not yet in force]

"(1) An integrated care board or NHS England may enter into a contract under which primary medical services are provided in accordance with the following provisions of this Part.

(2) A contract under this section is called in this Act a "general medical services contract"…"

Section 92: Arrangements by the Board for the provision of primary medical services

"(1) The Board may make agreements, other than arrangements pursuant to section 83(2) or general medical services contracts, under which primary medical services are provided.

> *(2) An agreement must be in accordance with regulations under section 94…"*

Section 92: Arrangements by an integrated care board or NHS England for the provision of primary medical services [not yet in force]

> *"(1) An integrated care board or NHS England may make agreements, other than arrangements pursuant to section 83 or general medical services contracts, under which primary medical services are provided.*
>
> *(2) An agreement must be in accordance with regulations under section 94…"*

Contracts for primary care services

There are three different types of contract for provision of primary care:[45]

- a general medical services ("GMS") contract, pursuant to section 84 above. This is subject to the NHS (General Medical Services Contracts) Regulations 2015. It is the national standard GP contract, and thus by far the most common type of contract;

- a personal medical services ("PMS") contract, pursuant to section 92 above. This is subject to the NHS (Personal

45 See https://www.england.nhs.uk/long-read/gp-contract/ [accessed 29 April 2024].

Medical Services Agreements) Regulations 2015. It is a locally agreed contract with GP practices;

- an alternative provider medical services ("APMS") contract, pursuant to section 83(2) above. This is subject to the Alternative Provider Medical Services Directions 2020. It is the least common type of contract and offers the most flexibility. It can be entered with private companies.

Indemnity for clinical negligence liabilities

The "NHS Indemnity" scheme was introduced on 1 January 1990; under its terms, health authorities became directly financially responsible for the clinical liabilities[46] of medical professionals employed by them. Before this, medical indemnity cover was provided by medical defence organisations ("MDOs"), which NHS doctors were required to pay for membership of. GPs were not covered by the scheme, unless (unusually) employed by a health authority and providing services as part of that employment. The scheme was introduced because of the increasing cost of membership of MDOs, costs which were largely paid for by health authorities, and concern that doctors from particular medical specialisms (such as obstetrics) could be subject to higher membership costs.[47]

The Clinical Negligence Scheme for Trusts (the "CNST") was established in England in 1995 under what is now section 71 of the NHS Act 2006 in order to handle clinical negligence claims and meet

---

46 That is, liabilities arising from clinical care

47 See *"NHS indemnity: the implications for medical litigation"* by Margaret Brazier (1990) 6 PN 88

their costs.[48] All NHS Trusts and NHS Foundation Trusts are currently members of the CNST, for which they pay contributions. The CNST is managed by the NHS Litigation Authority, which has been known as NHS Resolution ("NHSR") since 2017. The CNST is now governed by the NHS (Clinical Negligence Scheme) Regulations 2015. It is worth noting that under regulation 10 of those Regulations a member of the CNST, such as an NHS Trust, is indemnified for the clinical negligence of its subcontractors.[49]

Eligible healthcare bodies are also indemnified for clinical negligence claims in respect of incidents which occurred before 1 April 1995, pursuant to the NHS (Existing Liabilities Scheme) (England) Regulations 2018.

Many NHS hospital doctors still choose to be members of MDOs (the major MDOs being the Medical Defence Union ("MDU"), Medical Protection Society Limited ("MPS"), and Medical and Dental Defence Union of Scotland ("MDDUS")). The benefits of membership include access to legal advice and representation for the doctor,[50] indemnity cover for regulatory and disciplinary proceedings,

---

48 See https://resolution.nhs.uk/services/claims-management/clinical-schemes/clinical-negligence-scheme-for-trusts/ [accessed on 25 April 2024].

49 This does not, of course, affect whether a defendant NHS Trust is legally responsible for the negligence of its subcontractors, which will depend on a finding of vicarious liability or a non-delegable duty of care.

50 This is attractive given that claims are handled centrally by NHSR and doctors may be left feeling that claim outcomes are driven by commercial factors without regard to their personal professional interests.

and (importantly) indemnity cover for clinical negligence claims arising from private practice.

In 2019 the government assumed comprehensive liability for clinical negligence claims arising from NHS-funded general practice under the Clinical Negligence Scheme for General Practice (the "CNSGP"). This represented a major change, as GPs had historically arranged their own indemnity cover. It was driven in the author's view by the increased cost of membership of MDOs (resulting from the negative personal injury discount rate since 2017, which increased the value of personal injury claims), and concern among GPs that the quantum of a damages claim could exceed the limit of their indemnity cover, which was impacting recruitment and retention. The CNSGP was established by the NHS (Clinical Negligence Scheme for General Practice) Regulations 2019 and commenced on 1 April 2019. Liabilities incurred by GPs in respect of NHS-funded care before 1 April 2019 are indemnified by the state pursuant to the NHS (Existing Liabilities Scheme for General Practice) Regulations 2020[51].

Doctors and hospitals providing private healthcare or NHS dentistry arrange their own indemnity cover.[52] This might take the form of an insurance policy (under which the insurance company is bound to indemnify the policyholder subject to the contractual terms),

[51] This is subject to arrangements being in place between the relevant MDO and the Secretary of State.

[52] Appropriate indemnity cover has been compulsory for medical professionals since 2014: schedule 1(1) of the Health Care and Associated Professions (Indemnity Arrangements) Order 2014/1887.

membership of the CNST,[53] or (most commonly) membership of an MDO. Indemnity cover pursuant to membership of one of the three major MDOs is entirely discretionary: an MDO can refuse to cover the cost of a claim for any reason. The MDOs are also not subject to any regulation. This puts both doctors and patients at risk. It was brought to the government's attention by the 2020 Paterson Inquiry, which recommended reform to the current regulation of indemnity products and a nationwide safety net for patients.[54]

The Department for Health and Social Care ("DHSC") ran a consultation responding to this recommendation. Its preferred option was to legislate to ensure that all regulated professionals not covered by NHS indemnity have clinical negligence cover which is subject to regulation by the FCA (Financial Conduct Authority) and PRA (Prudential Regulation Authority). The main drawback identified to this was increased cost.

At the time of writing, no legislation has been enacted to give effect to the above recommendations. According to a parliamentary statement on 7 March 2024 MDOs have proposed to implement a code of practice to provide greater transparency around discretionary indemnity cover by the end of the year.[55]

---

53 Since April 2013 private healthcare providers have been allowed to join the CNST subject to payment of contributions.

54 The MDU refused cover for Ian Paterson's private patients on the basis that his acts were criminal.

55 https://questions-statements.parliament.uk/written-statements/detail/2024-03-07/hcws318 [accessed 25 April 2024]

CHAPTER NINE

PRACTICAL TIPS ON LITIGATING NON-DELEGABLE DUTIES

A dispute between parties as to the existence of a non-delegable duty of care should first be identified pre-action, at the stage of exchanging the Letter of Claim and Letter of Response.[56] The issue should fully crystalise in the Particulars of Claim and Defence.

The claimant should seek disclosure of the following (if applicable) from the defendant at the pre-action stage:

- contractual documents between the defendant and the health professional(s) (or other healthcare provider and/or relevant company);
- relevant policies and/or procedures governing the health professional's use of the hospital or other healthcare premises;

---

56 Pursuant to the Pre-Action Protocol for the Resolution of Clinical Disputes. See, for example, paragraphs 2.2(c) and (h).

- in the case of private healthcare, invoices for medical care, correspondence with the healthcare provider, the treatment plan, and contractual documents;[57]

- contractual documents between the defendant and an NHS healthcare body (such as an integrated care board) for provision of healthcare.

The defendant is likely to have control of the documents above. It should seek disclosure from the claimant of any medical records which it does not have access to.

The pleadings must set out the relevant facts, which will depend on the case, but might include:

- the claimant's attendance(s) at a hospital (or other healthcare premises) run by the defendant;

- the employment status of staff who attended to the claimant;

- relevant terms of any contract (whether between the claimant and the defendant, between the defendant and the relevant healthcare provider and/or company, or between the defendant and the NHS healthcare body (such as an integrated care board));

- relevant terms of any policy or procedure governing the health professional's use of the hospital or other healthcare premises;

---

[57] Assuming that the claimant has not retained those documents.

- relevant terms of the claimant's treatment plan.

The Particulars of Claim and Defence must state clearly that they contend, respectively, that a non-delegable duty of care is / is not owed. If a statutory provision is relied on as the basis of a non-delegable duty, that should be stated.

Part 18 requests for further information and Part 32.18 notices to admit facts should be used as appropriate. If a party fails to plead facts relevant to the existence of a non-delegable duty, and the basis of that party's pleading regarding the non-delegable duty point is unclear, the other side should consider a Part 18 request. If a party has a strong case in respect of the non-delegable duty point, and relevant facts have not been formally admitted by the other side, a notice to admit facts should be considered.

If the claimant is bringing a claim in respect of private healthcare or NHS dentistry, it would be prudent to ask the proposed defendant at the pre-action stage to confirm (a) which insurance company or MDO he or she is covered by, (b) that (if applicable) the MDO is covering the claim, and (c) whether there is any limit to the indemnity. The Pre-Action Protocol for the Resolution of Clinical Disputes anticipates that at the very least the name of the indemnity insurer should be shared.[58] If the defendant fails to respond adequately to the claimant's queries, and the claimant has grounds for concern that the defendant is uninsured or under-insured, there are limited options to compel the defendant to provide the information. A Part 18 request may be made, but there are conflicting High Court authorities as to whether questions about the nature and extent of insurance cover are

---

[58] Paragraph 3.24(h).

within the remit of Part 18, if insurance is not at issue in the claim.[59] The general consensus is that they are not. The Court may order a defendant to provide a witness statement setting out whether it has adequate insurance to fund its participation in the litigation to trial under CPR rule 3.1(2)(m), because that is relevant to case management, but not whether it has adequate insurance to meet an award of damages and costs. The claimant will therefore have to make a decision, if concerned about whether the proposed defendant has adequate insurance, whether to bring a claim against him nonetheless, or to bring a claim (in addition, or instead) against a body which arguably owes a non-delegable duty of care.

A defendant to a claim in which there is likely to be a finding of a non-delegable duty of care should consider bringing a Part 20 claim for a contribution or indemnity; alternatively a claim against the negligent third party under the Civil Liability (Contribution) Act 1978, following settlement or judgment. Where the allegedly negligent third party is a GP or other NHS body, they will be covered by the NHS indemnity, removing the need for a claim against them by another NHS body.[60]

If the claim hinges on the discrete issue of whether the defendant owed the claimant a non-delegable duty of care, it may be appropriate for the existence of a non-delegable duty to be tried as a preliminary

---

59 See *Harcourt v Griffin* [2007] EWHC 1500 (QB); [2007] P.I.Q.R Q9, *West London Pipeline & Storage Ltd v Total UK Ltd* [2008] EWHC 1296 (Comm); [2008] Lloyd's Rep. I.R. 688 and *XYZ v Various sub nom Re Breast Implant Litigation* [2013] EWHC 3643 (QB); [2014] 2 Costs L.O. 197.

60 Cf *Medical Negligence*, Jones, 6th edition, at paragraph 9-090

issue[61]. If facts relevant to the non-delegable duty are heavily disputed, the preliminary issue trial will need to hear oral evidence. The parties should agree a schedule of agreed and disputed facts (alternatively, agreed or assumed facts if there is not to be oral evidence) in advance, covering everything relevant to the existence of a non-delegable duty of care.

61 See the guidance of David Steele J in *McLoughlin v Grovers (A Firm)* [2001] EWCA Civ 1743; [2002] Q.B. 1312 at paragraph 66.

MORE BOOKS BY LAW BRIEF PUBLISHING

A selection of our other titles available now:-

'A Practical Guide to the Independent School Standards – September 2023 Edition' by Sarah McKimm
'A Practical Guide to Estate Administration and Crypto Assets' by Richard Marshall
'A Practical Guide to Managing GDPR Data Subject Access Requests – Second Edition' by Patrick O'Kane
'A Practical Guide to Parental Alienation in Private and Public Law Children Cases' by Sam King QC & Frankie Shama
'Contested Heritage – Removing Art from Land and Historic Buildings' by Richard Harwood QC, Catherine Dobson, David Sawtell
'The Limits of Separate Legal Personality: When Those Running a Company Can Be Held Personally Liable for Losses Caused to Third Parties Outside of the Company' by Dr Mike Wilkinson
'A Practical Guide to Transgender Law' by Robin Moira White & Nicola Newbegin
'A Practical Guide to 'Stranded Spouses' in Family Law' by Mani Singh Basi
'A Practical Guide to Residential Freehold Conveyancing' by Lorraine Richardson
'A Practical Guide to Pensions on Divorce for Lawyers' by Bryan Scant
'A Practical Guide to Challenging Sham Marriage Allegations in Immigration Law' by Priya Solanki
'A Practical Guide to Digital Communications Evidence in Criminal Law' by Sam Willis
'A Practical Guide to Legal Rights in Scotland' by Sarah-Jane Macdonald
'A Practical Guide to New Build Conveyancing' by Paul Sams & Rebecca East
'A Practical Guide to Defending Barristers in Disciplinary Cases' by Marc Beaumont
'A Practical Guide to Inherited Wealth on Divorce' by Hayley Trim
'A Practical Guide to Practice Direction 12J and Domestic Abuse in Private Law Children Proceedings' by Rebecca Cross & Malvika Jaganmohan

'A Practical Guide to Confiscation and Restraint' by Narita Bahra QC, John Carl Townsend, David Winch
'A Practical Guide to the Law of Forests in Scotland' by Philip Buchan
'A Practical Guide to Health and Medical Cases in Immigration Law' by Rebecca Chapman & Miranda Butler
'A Practical Guide to Bad Character Evidence for Criminal Practitioners by Aparna Rao
'A Practical Guide to Extradition Law post-Brexit' by Myles Grandison et al
'A Practical Guide to Hoarding and Mental Health for Housing Lawyers' by Rachel Coyle
'A Practical Guide to Psychiatric Claims in Personal Injury – 2nd Edition' by Liam Ryan
'Stephens on Contractual Indemnities' by Richard Stephens
'A Practical Guide to the EU Succession Regulation' by Richard Frimston
'A Practical Guide to Solicitor and Client Costs – 2nd Edition' by Robin Dunne
'Constructive Dismissal – Practice Pointers and Principles' by Benjimin Burgher
'A Practical Guide to Religion and Belief Discrimination Claims in the Workplace' by Kashif Ali
'A Practical Guide to the Law of Medical Treatment Decisions' by Ben Troke
'Fundamental Dishonesty and QOCS in Personal Injury Proceedings: Law and Practice' by Jake Rowley
'A Practical Guide to the Law in Relation to School Exclusions' by Charlotte Hadfield & Alice de Coverley
'A Practical Guide to Divorce for the Silver Separators' by Karin Walker
'The Right to be Forgotten – The Law and Practical Issues' by Melissa Stock
'A Practical Guide to Planning Law and Rights of Way in National Parks, the Broads and AONBs' by James Maurici QC, James Neill et al
'A Practical Guide to Election Law' by Tom Tabori
'A Practical Guide to the Law in Relation to Surrogacy' by Andrew Powell
'A Practical Guide to Claims Arising from Fatal Accidents – 2nd Edition' by James Patience
'A Practical Guide to the Ownership of Employee Inventions – From Entitlement to Compensation' by James Tumbridge & Ashley Roughton
'A Practical Guide to Asbestos Claims' by Jonathan Owen & Gareth McAloon

'A Practical Guide to Stamp Duty Land Tax in England and Northern Ireland' by Suzanne O'Hara
'A Practical Guide to the Law of Farming Partnerships' by Philip Whitcomb
'Covid-19, Homeworking and the Law – The Essential Guide to Employment and GDPR Issues' by Forbes Solicitors
'Covid-19 and Criminal Law – The Essential Guide' by Ramya Nagesh
'Covid-19 and Family Law in England and Wales – The Essential Guide' by Safda Mahmood
'A Practical Guide to the Law of Unlawful Eviction and Harassment – 2nd Edition' by Stephanie Lovegrove
'Covid-19, Brexit and the Law of Commercial Leases – The Essential Guide' by Mark Shelton
'A Practical Guide to Costs in Personal Injury Claims – 2nd Edition' by Matthew Hoe
'A Practical Guide to the General Data Protection Regulation (GDPR) – 2nd Edition' by Keith Markham
'Ellis on Credit Hire – Sixth Edition' by Aidan Ellis & Tim Kevan
'A Practical Guide to Working with Litigants in Person and McKenzie Friends in Family Cases' by Stuart Barlow
'Protecting Unregistered Brands: A Practical Guide to the Law of Passing Off' by Lorna Brazell
'A Practical Guide to Secondary Liability and Joint Enterprise Post-Jogee' by Joanne Cecil & James Mehigan
'A Practical Guide to the Pre-Action RTA Claims Protocol for Personal Injury Lawyers' by Antonia Ford
'A Practical Guide to Neighbour Disputes and the Law' by Alexander Walsh
'A Practical Guide to Forfeiture of Leases' by Mark Shelton
'A Practical Guide to Coercive Control for Legal Practitioners and Victims' by Rachel Horman
'A Practical Guide to the Law of Driverless Cars – Second Edition' by Alex Glassbrook, Emma Northey & Scarlett Milligan
'A Practical Guide to TOLATA Claims' by Greg Williams
'A Practical Guide to Elderly Law – 2nd Edition' by Justin Patten
'A Practical Guide to Responding to Housing Disrepair and Unfitness Claims' by Iain Wightwick

'A Practical Guide to the Law of Bullying and Harassment in the Workplace' by Philip Hyland
'How to Be a Freelance Solicitor: A Practical Guide to the SRA-Regulated Freelance Solicitor Model' by Paul Bennett
'A Practical Guide to Prison Injury Claims' by Malcolm Johnson
'A Practical Guide to the Small Claims Track – 2nd Edition' by Dominic Bright
'A Practical Guide to Advising Clients at the Police Station' by Colin Stephen McKeown-Beaumont
'A Practical Guide to Antisocial Behaviour Injunctions' by Iain Wightwick
'Practical Mediation: A Guide for Mediators, Advocates, Advisers, Lawyers, and Students in Civil, Commercial, Business, Property, Workplace, and Employment Cases' by Jonathan Dingle with John Sephton
'The Mini-Pupillage Workbook' by David Boyle
'A Practical Guide to Crofting Law' by Brian Inkster
'A Practical Guide to the Law of Domain Names and Cybersquatting' by Andrew Clemson
'A Practical Guide to the Law of Gender Pay Gap Reporting' by Harini Iyengar
'NHS Whistleblowing and the Law' by Joseph England
'Employment Law and the Gig Economy' by Nigel Mackay & Annie Powell
'A Practical Guide to Noise Induced Hearing Loss (NIHL) Claims' by Andrew Mckie, Ian Skeate, Gareth McAloon
'An Introduction to Beauty Negligence Claims – A Practical Guide for the Personal Injury Practitioner' by Greg Almond
'Intercompany Agreements for Transfer Pricing Compliance' by Paul Sutton
'Zen and the Art of Mediation' by Martin Plowman
'A Practical Guide to the SRA Principles, Individual and Law Firm Codes of Conduct 2019 – What Every Law Firm Needs to Know' by Paul Bennett
'A Practical Guide to Adoption for Family Lawyers' by Graham Pegg
'A Practical Guide to Industrial Disease Claims' by Andrew Mckie & Ian Skeate
'A Practical Guide to Conducting a Sheriff Court Proof' by Andrew Stevenson
'A Practical Guide to Vicarious Liability' by Mariel Irvine
'A Practical Guide to Applications for Landlord's Consent and Variation of Leases' by Mark Shelton
'A Practical Guide to Relief from Sanctions Post-Mitchell and Denton' by Peter Causton

'A Practical Guide to Equity Release for Advisors' by Paul Sams
'A Practical Guide to Financial Services Claims' by Chris Hegarty
'The Law of Houses in Multiple Occupation: A Practical Guide to HMO Proceedings' by Julian Hunt
'Occupiers, Highways and Defective Premises Claims: A Practical Guide Post-Jackson – 2nd Edition' by Andrew Mckie
'A Practical Guide to Financial Ombudsman Service Claims' by Adam Temple & Robert Scrivenor
'A Practical Guide to Running Housing Disrepair and Cavity Wall Claims: 2nd Edition' by Andrew Mckie & Ian Skeate
'A Practical Guide to Holiday Sickness Claims – 2nd Edition' by Andrew Mckie & Ian Skeate
'Arguments and Tactics for Personal Injury and Clinical Negligence Claims' by Dorian Williams
'A Practical Guide to Drone Law' by Rufus Ballaster, Andrew Firman, Eleanor Clot
'A Practical Guide to Compliance for Personal Injury Firms Working With Claims Management Companies' by Paul Bennett
'RTA Allegations of Fraud in a Post-Jackson Era: The Handbook – 2nd Edition' by Andrew Mckie
'RTA Personal Injury Claims: A Practical Guide Post-Jackson' by Andrew Mckie
'On Experts: CPR35 for Lawyers and Experts' by David Boyle
'An Introduction to Personal Injury Law' by David Boyle

These books and more are available to order online direct from the publisher at www.lawbriefpublishing.com, where you can also read free sample chapters. For any queries, contact us on 0844 587 2383 or mail@lawbriefpublishing.com.

Our books are also usually in stock at www.amazon.co.uk with free next day delivery for Prime members, and at good legal bookshops such as Wildy & Sons.

We are regularly launching new books in our series of practical day-to-day practitioners' guides. Visit our website and join our free newsletter to be kept informed and to receive special offers, free chapters, etc.

You can also follow us on Twitter at www.twitter.com/lawbriefpub.

www.ingramcontent.com/pod-product-compliance
Ingram Content Group UK Ltd.
Pitfield, Milton Keynes, MK11 3LW, UK
UKHW020151290926
15471UKWH00004B/801

9 781916 698345